BENEFICIARIES
OF GRACE

BENEFICIARIES OF GRACE

DEBOLA AJAYI

Baal Hamon Publishers

Akure   London   New York

© 2019, Debola Ajayi

All rights reserved. The rights of Debola Ajayi to be identified as the copyright holder of this work has been asserted. No part of this publication may be reproduced, stored in a retrieval system or transmitted in any way by any means, electronic, mechanical, photocopy, recording or otherwise, without the prior permission of the copyright holder except as provided by the copyright laws of England. Unless otherwise noted, all scriptures quoted in this book are taken from the Holy Bible, King James Version (KJV).

ISBN-13: 978-1-9999266-3-2

International Correspondence:

www.baalhamonpublishers.com

publishers@baalhamon.com

The author may be contacted via:

Email: debolamary76@gmail.com

or   maajayi@futa.edu.ng

Tel: (+234) 0803 4180 077

WhatsApp: (+234) 0803 4180 077

CONTENTS

Dedication		vii
Acknowledgement		Ix
Foreword		xvii
Preface		xxi
Chapter One	**The Woman with the Spirit of Infirmity:** *Living in Her Own Shadow*	1
Chapter Two	**The Woman with the Issue of Blood:** *With A Will And A Way*	13
Chapter Three	**The Daughter of Jairus:** *Enjoying the Faith of A Father*	23
Chapter Four	**The Daughter of the Syrophenician Woman:** *Blessed With A Persistent Mum*	33
Chapter Five	**The Mother In-Law of Simon Peter:** *Laid Down But Raised To Serve*	45
Chapter Six	**Mary Magdalene:** *Transformed And Ever Loving*	53
Chapter Seven	**The Samaritan Woman:** *Thirsty for Satisfaction*	65
Chapter Eight	**The Woman Caught in Adultery:** *Saved To Sin No More*	77
Chapter Nine	**My Personal Testimony**	85
Chapter Ten	**Final Words**	107

DEDICATION

This book is dedicated to Jesus Christ my Saviour, Lord, Friend and Healer and to everyone who has benefited from His amazing grace.

ACKNOWLEDGEMENTS

With special thanks:

To Pastor Olusegun Blessed Ajayi, my one and only darling husband, for your constant support that provided the enabling environment to write and publish this book. Your leadership and total loving care have given me the opportunity to manifest all my God-given potentials and added colour to my life. Thank you for always being there with words of encouragement, challenge, hope, inspiration and godly counsels especially at the time of passing through the valley of the shadow of death.

To my father in the Lord, Pastor (Prof.) Samuel O. Ewuola, whose life has always challenged me in every aspect. In his 70s, he is still writing and publishing books. Thank you, Daddy, for being such an inspiration and allowing yourself to be used of the Lord to provide the needed assurance from the Lord that has carried me above every wind of sorrow and fear. You have been a strong support in my life which I will never forget.

To my father in the Lord, Venerable (Prof.) Akin Lasehinde, for being there, always standing by us in every situation. Your life is an example worthy of emulation; still bearing fruits in old age too, writing and publishing books in your 70s. I specially thank you for accepting to read through this book at short notice despite your schedules, for the suggestion that I should add my personal testimony and for writing the Foreword.

To all my fathers and mothers in the Lord in my home church, Pastor and Mrs E. O. Oluwanimotele, the Regional Pastor of the Gospel Faith Mission International (GOFAMINT), Region 3; Pastor (Prof) and Prof (Mrs) A. A. Olufayo, the District Pastor of GOFAMINT, Obanla District; and my Assembly Pastor of the GOFAMINT Pacesetters Assembly, Pastor (Dr) and Mrs D. B. Ilori and all the ministers,

Acknowledgements

workers and members, for their huge and unquantifiable support while with them and while away on assignment with my husband at the Chapel of Faith, FUTA. Thank you for not forgetting to stand by us through thick and thin.

To all my fathers and mothers, brothers and sisters in the Lord in the Chapel of Faith, FUTA; for your love displayed by the prayer chains, giving and every form of support before, during and after the period of sickness. What could I have done without God and you? You are too numerous to be mentioned. I specially acknowledge the Chairman (Prof. A. A. Taiwo) and members of the Chapel Council for the financial support and the leaders of the Women's Fellowship especially Mummy 'Motunde Fagbenro for the nights spent sleeping on a chair in the hospital with me for almost two weeks and arranging for my feeding. I thank Brother Dayo Popoola and his bride Sister Mercy Popoola for volunteering to be my PA, following me to hospital each time for treatment and looking after my children during the long vacation when I was away. I thank the Chapel "Pilot," Brother Alabede, for all the hospital and other runs. I appreciate the Daddies and the youths for their immense support, and the Chapel children too for being so understanding enough not to stream in after church services to disturb when I was on the sick bed, and for their prayers and get-well-soon wishes. You are all wonderful.

To the Vice Chancellor of the Federal University of Technology Akure, Prof J. A Fuwape, a beloved father in the Chapel, who supported immensely in different dimensions. God bless you, sir.

To my amiable Dean of the School of Environmental Technology, Prof. I.B. Kashim, my beloved Head of Department of Estate Management, Dr M.B. Ogunleye and all my noble colleagues, for rallying round me and supporting in innumerable ways.

To the "Comrade Chair," Dr 'Bola Oniya, and the executives of the Academic Staff Union of University (ASUU) FUTA Branch for the financial support and visit during the crisis.

To all my Pastor friends, brothers and sisters, alumni of the GOFAMINT Students' Fellowship, FUTA, and at the national level; for the demonstration of love and

Acknowledgements

support. You are too numerous to be mentioned by name, God bless you all.

To Pastor and Mrs. R. T. Ologbonyo and their children (Charis Generation Church, Ibadan) for the immeasurable support, especially at the peak of the medical treatment at the University College Hospital, Ibadan.

To all the medical personnel in the Chapel of Faith, FUTA and in GOFAMINT, Pacesetters Assembly, (Daddy and Mummy Akin Odetola of St David's Hospital, (for the constant pain relieving injections and tablets and for the professional counsels and connections), Dr Ericson Omolade (for the diagnosis of the eye defects and the glasses and also the professional connections), Mummy Beatrice Attoye (for dressing my surgery wounds), Sister Ayodele Ewemooje and Mummy Moromoke Olasende (for the post treatment physiotherapy check-ups and medical advice) and Deacon Segun Owoseeni of Alpha Medical Laboratory Services, Gbogi, Akure (for the free blood tests and constantly checking on me).

Beneficiaries of Grace

To my beloved Oncologist, Dr Ndidi Okunuga of University of Medical Sciences Teaching Hospital, Akure (for being both professional and caring), Dr Chuks Efonyeaku of Mishmael Specialist Hospital, Oba-Ile, Akure and Dr B. A. Yusuf of University College Hospital, Ibadan for your professional expertise.

To my beloved family members: (sisters, brother, mother-in-law, brothers- and sisters- in-law, nieces, nephews and cousins) and others too numerous to mention (for the financial, spiritual, moral, material and physical support) and to my dear sons, Promise and Peculiar, and my dear daughter, Praise for being my PAs.

To the members of Team Survivors Nigeria, who stood by me in the joint struggle and victory, especially Mrs Funmi Oluwagbamila. I use this medium to appreciate Her Excellency, Mrs Betty Anyanwu–Akeredolu, wife of the Ondo State Governor, for her enlightenment campaigns and encouragement to cancer patients.

Acknowledgements

To the members and executives of the Organisation for Women in Science for the Developing World (OWSD) FUTA Chapter, under the capable leadership of Professor T.T. Adebolu, for the financial and moral support. We are more than conquerors through Christ.

To my Max family, especially Pastor Roberts Adebisi and Mr Akinola Akinjuyigbe, for the constant supply of supplements.

To Evangelist Bunmi Monehin (GOFAMINT) for the initial proofreading and restructuring of this book and to Brother Temitope Oyetomi, (Chapel of Faith, FUTA) for offering to design the book.

To Sister Aladesanmi Blessing (for holding on the coordination of the Virtuous Girls' Club meetings for me through the months of my non-availability); to all the members of the Virtuous Girls' Club and their parents in Asuwamo Estate, Aule, Akure. Thank you for your prayers, visits and kind assistance in your own ways. I know you are one of the reasons why God spared my life.

Beneficiaries of Grace

To all my neighbours, friends and acquaintances within and outside the FUTA community who heard of my medical condition and dared to pray, called, visited and gave in cash and in kind. Sounds of joy shall not cease in our homes in Jesus' name.

To everyone that God used to help me to scale through to sound health and have the quality of life to complete this book.

FOREWORD

Grace is often taken for granted. If you go to a busy hospital, you will better appreciate God's grace of good health you are enjoying than when you are in the midst of healthy, hale and hearty crowd of people on the streets. The author, Dr. (Mrs) Debola Ajayi, has thoughtfully given attention to eight women in the Bible who went through trying challenges, mostly health-wise and survived through grace. It is understandable that she focused on women because she is also a woman. She analysed each case scripturally, examining the personality of the woman concerned and diagnosed her peculiar problem or problems. The unique healing method by the Lord Jesus Christ for each of the cases requiring healing was well discussed. She showed clearly that our Lord is unlimited in methods of attending to challenges as she brilliantly compared scriptures. It is incisive and worth reading.

Dr. (Mrs) Ajayi did not confine herself to highlighting the problems and solutions for each case, she took time to show the reactions of people around each case that benefited from grace. Ironically in many instances, rather than rejoicing, many were either jealous of the recipient or indignant about the intervention of Jesus in helping. For each case, personal applications which will benefit every reader were clearly stated. Most of the relevant scriptures cited were written out to facilitate smooth reading such that the reader is not distracted from opening the Bible. Each chapter is captivating, indeed very interesting to read without any boredom.

The last but one chapter (Chapter Nine) contains the author's personal detailed testimony of how she was a beneficiary of grace which is the title of her book. It was a serious war with cancer and she won by GRACE. The value of human life can be vividly seen in this testimony. An average reader will wonder that a woman who went through the unbelievable destructive blow of the enemy on her health could bounce back to write this excellent book. Life is valuable. The enemy is very wicked, but our God is very gracious.

This author's testimony is worth publishing as a separate small book but she has sourced this book with it. One can say that any reader who misses this chapter has missed much of the book. I consider it a privilege to write the Foreword. I congratulate the author for contributing this work to humanity and I commend the book to every reader for abundant spiritual blessings.

Ven. (Prof.) Akin Laseinde (Rtd)
Emeritus Chaplain,
The Chapel of Faith,
Federal University of Technology, Akure.

PREFACE

My interest in gender analysis made me to look at the gender spread of people who were healed by Jesus Christ during His earthly ministry. It was interesting to note that Jesus healed more men than women but the cases of the women were so interesting to me that I decided to write on them. After the completion of my Ph. D in 2014, I started writing until I was halted by a diagnosis of breast cancer in August 2015. I wanted the book to come out in 2016 to mark my 40th birthday but I was discouraged or I discouraged myself, to continue the writing. How can I write on Jesus' healing power when I was battling with breast cancer? However, I resumed and completed the nine chapters of the book in 2017 and was planning on publishing it when the battle began again in a greater dimension. Thank God who always causes us to triumph; His grace carried me through and added a new chapter to the book, which is my personal testimony.

This book focuses on women who benefited from the amazing grace of Jesus during his earthly ministry and became liberated from the shackles of sickness, satanic oppression and sin. The woman is the crown of all creation, that is, the last of God's creation. She is the cause of the fall and also the vessel of salvation through which the Saviour of mankind was born. Her creation and existence is very significant to the plan and purpose of God. God promised that the seed of the woman will bruise the head of the serpent, the Devil (Genesis 3: 15). Little wonder then that the Devil, the arch-enemy of the human race always seeks to make life miserable for the woman and hold her in captivity to prevent the full expression of her God - given abilities.

Since the fall of man, the devil has afflicted the human race with sin, sorrow, sickness, slavery. Men and women have long been held captives and broken-hearted due to many societal ills such as abuse, addiction, violence, poverty, diseases, and demonic afflictions among others. All of these hold the captives in bondage and keep them living below the standards of purity, joy, peace, health, wealth, marital bliss and

Preface

fulfilment in life. Jesus Christ came to bind up the broken-hearted and proclaim liberty to the captives. Jesus Christ became flesh so we can behold His glory, as of the only begotten of the Father. He was full of grace and truth and from His fullness we have all received grace. (John 1:14, 16). He came to make us beneficiaries of His grace so that our lives can reflect his glory. Grace and glory go together. Psalm 84:11b says "…the Lord will give grace and glory….." The only thing that can make a life beautiful and glorious is the grace of Jesus. He alone can give grace and glory. We all need His grace. When a life experiences grace, glory follows.

The word "grace" has commonly been defined by Christians as **God's Riches At Christ's Expense.** Grace is an unmerited favour enjoyed from God. It is God doing for us what we in no way deserve. Grace was first mentioned in the Bible with respect to Noah. "But Noah found grace in the eyes of the Lord" (Genesis 6:8). When the whole earth was swept off with a flood, grace exempted only Noah and his family. Grace has an all-encompassing effect that cuts across realms of the spiritual, emotional, psychological, social and physical. Freedom from social disgrace, inferiority complex, discrimination, fear, lack, oppression, sickness and sin are all entailed in the total package brought to mankind through the amazing grace of Jesus Christ.

This package of grace is available and free for all without discrimination on the basis of gender, age, race, religion or class. I have enjoyed this grace and I invite you my dear reader to enjoy the fullness of grace that is available in Jesus Christ. May you receive a touch of His grace as you read through the experiences of these women (including mine) who were beneficiaries of the amazing grace of Jesus Christ. May you hear his voice proclaiming liberty to any area of captivity in your life. Amen.

CHAPTER ONE

THE WOMAN WITH THE SPIRIT OF INFIRMITY
Living in Her Own Shadow

The account of this woman whose name was not significant enough to be mentioned, can be found only in the Gospel of Luke, chapter 13, verse 10 through 17 which reads:

> *"And he was teaching in one of the synagogues on the Sabbath. And, behold, there was a woman which had a spirit of infirmity eighteen years, and was bowed together, and could in no wise lift up herself. And when Jesus saw her, he called her to him, and said unto her, Woman, thou art loosed from thine infirmity. And he laid his hands on her: and immediately she was made straight, and glorified God.*
>
> *And the ruler of the synagogue answered with indignation, because that Jesus had healed on the*

Sabbath day, and said unto the people, There are six days in which men ought to work: in them therefore come and be healed, and not on the Sabbath day.

The Lord then answered him and said thou hypocrite, doth not each one of you on the Sabbath loose his ox or his ass from the stall and lead him away to watering? And ought not this woman, being a daughter of Abraham whom Satan hath bound, lo, these eighteen years be loosed from this bond on the Sabbath day?

And when he said these things, all his adversaries were ashamed: and all the people rejoiced for all the glorious things that were done by him."

Her Personality and Problem

The recipient of this work of grace was an Israelite woman, a faithful worshipper who had gathered with other Israelites to worship God despite her condition. This middle-aged woman did not use her affliction as an excuse for disobeying the fourth commandment, which is to keep the Sabbath day holy. She must have been going regularly to the synagogue before the day that Jesus healed her. Her faithfulness in obeying the fourth commandment was rewarded on this glorious Sabbath as she bent there listening to the gracious words that proceeded from the mouth of Jesus. Although she was a daughter of Abraham, an heiress to the commonwealth of Israel, she was not enjoying the benefits of being a daughter of Abraham. Her health was impaired and perhaps her finances too, as sickness and poverty often go together.

Liberty must be proclaimed and the captive must hear it. If not proclaimed, the captive will remain in his captivity not knowing that a higher power has set him free.

Despite being an heiress or a daughter of Abraham, this woman was bound by the devil for almost two decades. Her case was beyond natural deformity, she was under oppression and captivity by the spirit of infirmity. She was bent doubled or *"bowed*

together, and could in no wise lift up herself". She could not lift herself up; her lifting up requires divine intervention. For good eighteen years, she has been under this infirmity. Although the Bible was silent about her age, eighteen years in the life of a woman would have taken up most, if not all of her reproductive years. This implies that if she was unmarried before the infirmity set in, say 16 years old, she may remain an old maid throughout life because the prospect of having a happy married life would almost be eluding her. Her case was quite a pathetic one.

The *height* of this woman was shortened. She could not arise to attain the heights God has destined her to reach in life. Whatever her dreams in life were, a blissful matrimony and a blossoming business enterprise, they remained only in the realms of her imaginations and could find no expression or actualization. Also, her *horizon* was limited. Her horizon was limited to seeing things that are below. She could neither lift up her eyes to the hills nor behold the beauty of the sky, the sun, the moon and the stars. All she could see was the ground and her own shadow. She lived a shadow of her real self, a distortion of the beauty God had made her to be. This woman continued living a life less than what God had designed for her.

Meanwhile, do not neglect your spiritual exercises and ministry because of what you are going through that may be unpalatable.

Her Healing

The law and religious observance could do nothing to alleviate the suffering and social discrimination that this woman went through. Thank God for grace that came through the Lord Jesus Christ, the grace that sets free from all forms of bondage! As Jesus was teaching on that glorious day, the condition of this woman attracted His attention. She was probably among the first arrivals and in the front row for Jesus to have seen her while teaching. He saw her and had mercy on her. He took the initiative for the healing and made her a beneficiary of His grace, even without her asking for it. What a grace!

> *"And when Jesus saw her, he called her to him, and said unto her, Woman, thou art loosed from thine infirmity. And he laid his hands on her: and immediately she was made straight, and glorified God".* (Luke 13: 12 – 13)

The Lord Jesus had to employ both means of voice and touch to set her free probably because her case was beyond natural deformity. He proclaimed liberty to her captivity and loosed her from the spirit of infirmity by saying ***"Woman, thou art loosed from thine infirmity"***. He went further to lay His hands on her and immediately, without further delay, she stood straight and glorified God for setting her free. She could then stand tall and lift her eyes and her hands to heaven glorifying God. What a relief! Of a truth ***"The Lord upholdeth all that fall, and raiseth up all those that be bowed down"*** (Psalm 145:14).

Liberty must be proclaimed and the captive must hear it. If not proclaimed, the captive will remain in his captivity not knowing that a higher power has set him free. If a Governor gives amnesty to a prisoner but the prisoner is not aware of it, nor understand its implication, he will continue his prison term. That is why Jesus declared in his manifesto in Luke 4:18-19 what was in Isaiah 61:1-3:

> *"The Spirit of the Lord God is upon me; because the Lord hath anointed me to preach good tidings unto the meek; he hath sent me to bind up the brokenhearted, to proclaim liberty to the captives, and the opening of prisons to them that are bound."*

In healing this woman, Jesus employed both the sound of his voice and the touch of his hands. Binding up of broken hearts may involve touch while proclamation of liberty is done with the voice. The good news is that as many as believe in Him have been set free from whatever holds us bound. All that is required is to appropriate the liberty He has proclaimed and make it a reality in our own lives through faith in His name (Acts 3:16).

Mixed Reactions

That is not the end of the story. For every work of grace there are always two reactions: appreciation and anger or indignation, praise and persecution or glorification and grumbling. As this woman glorified God, she was alone in the glorification. Her fellow worshippers were amazed but unable to join her in praising God for fear of the law that forbids doing any work on the Sabbath. Note the ungracious pronouncement from the mouth of the keeper of religious instructions:

> *"And the ruler of the synagogue answered with indignation, because that Jesus had healed on the Sabbath day, and said unto the people, There are six days in which men ought to work: in them therefore come and be healed, and not on the Sabbath day."* (Luke 13: 14)

His reaction was anger. He could not see beyond the strict observance of the law to rejoice with his synagogue member for her healing. Not everyone appreciates the work of grace, even today. Beneficiaries of grace however cannot but praise Him for the riches of his grace.

The Woman with the Spirit of Infirmity

"The Lord then answered him and said thou hypocrite, doth not each one of you on the Sabbath loose his ox or his ass from the stall and lead him away to watering? And ought not this woman, being a daughter of Abraham whom Satan hath bound, lo, these eighteen years be loosed from this bond on the Sabbath day? And when he said these things, all his adversaries were ashamed: and all the people rejoiced for all the glorious things that were done by him". (Luke 13: 15 – 17)

May God silence all your enemies so that your friends can join you to glorify God for making you a beneficiary of His grace. This woman was totally liberated from the spirit of infirmity. She was made whole by the power in the voice and touch of Jesus. Her obedience to the fourth commandment to keep the Sabbath day holy was rewarded with healing. It is true indeed that God has not called the House of Jacob to seek Him in vain. Whatever it is that is making you bow down, unable to live your life to the fullest to actualize your dreams, every infirmity holding you bound and making you live a shadow of your real person is broken by the power of His divine touch in Jesus name. Contact His grace and rise up to be whom

God has made you to be. His grace is still available today to lift up every one, man or woman that is bowed down.

Meanwhile, do not neglect your spiritual exercises and ministry because of what you are going through that may be unpalatable.

Personal Application

Are you a daughter of Abraham and going through tough times in your health, family, finance, career or business? Just keep holding on, wait upon your God because he is a faithful God (Isaiah 50:10). The Lord will surely liberate you from every condition that has kept you from living the abundant life in Christ. Meanwhile, do not neglect your spiritual exercises and ministry because of what you are going through that may be unpalatable. It has come to pass; that is, that condition will pass away just as it has come. You will soon be singing a brand new song of praise to God and all your enemies will be silenced and put to shame in Jesus' name. They will even be forced to join you to celebrate.

There are many men and women today who are bowed together under the weight of sickness, addiction, demonic oppression or the guilt of a sinful lifestyle. Such people cannot lift themselves up or deliver themselves from the yoke of bondage. They require a greater power to lift them up and that is found only in Jesus Christ. Jesus is still saying today *"Woman, thou art loosed."* He desires liberty, freedom, total liberation for everyone, either man or woman. He is willing and able to make you free and whole from every shackle put on you by evil forces, society, or persons. His liberty is total. ***"If the Son therefore shall make you free, ye shall be free indeed"*** (John 8:36). This healing represents the work of Christ's grace upon the soul. When crooked souls are made straight, God is glorified. We were once bowed together for a number of years by sin and Satan and unable to lift up ourselves until Jesus power and grace came. When a soul encounters the grace of salvation, there is joy unspeakable and full of glory. Are you still bent down with sin? Let the Son lift you up and make you free indeed.

This healing represents the work of Christ's grace upon the soul. When crooked souls are made straight, God is glorified.

CHAPTER TWO

THE WOMAN WITH THE ISSUE OF BLOOD
With A Will and A Way

The account of the woman with the issue of blood can be found in the three synoptic Gospels. For the purpose of this book, the account of the story in Mark 5: 25-34 shall be taken:

> *"And a certain woman, which had an issue of blood twelve years, And had suffered many things of many physicians, and had spent all that she had, and was nothing bettered, but rather grew worse, When she heard of Jesus, came in the press behind, and touched his garment. For she said, If I may touch but his clothes, I shall be whole. And straightway the fountain of her blood was dried up; and she felt in her body that she was healed of that plague.*

And Jesus, immediately knowing in himself that virtue had gone out of him, turned him about in the press, and said, Who touched my clothes?

And his disciples said unto him, Thou seest the multitude thronging thee, and sayest thou, Who touched me?

And he looked round about to see her that had done this thing. But the woman fearing and trembling, knowing what was done in her, came and fell down before him, and told him all the truth.

And he said unto her, Daughter, thy faith hath made thee whole; go in peace, and be whole of thy plague."

The Setting and the Problem

The setting of this story was the road from the Sea of Galilee. Jesus had just crossed over from the country of the Gadarenes where He had cast out a legion of unclean spirits from a mad man into a swine (verse 1 – 21). He was on His way to the house of Jairus, a ruler of the synagogue whose daughter was critically ill. There was a multitude of people following and pressing on Jesus as He went.

The Woman with the Issue of Blood

The woman with the issue of blood was an Israelite but by the nature of her disease was not allowed into the temple or synagogue because she was "unclean". According to Leviticus 15: 19 -31, she was to be separated or banned from coming to the tabernacle until the issue stopped. Hence, this woman did not have access to listen to the teachings of Jesus in the synagogue. She however had heard of Jesus, the miracle worker; and by hearing she had faith to be healed. When she saw the multitudes following Jesus on the way to Jairus' house, she seized the opportunity to reach out and tap her own miracle.

The case of this woman was a medical one with no spiritual undertone unlike the woman with the spirit of infirmity. An issue of blood or haemorrhage was not an uncommon medical condition but this woman's case was a prolonged one. For twelve solid years, one hundred and forty four months, the blood kept flowing without stopping. What a case! Everywhere she went, she was with sanitary pads. Her medical condition made her to become a *prey* to many doctors, going from one doctor to the other. The Bible says **"she had suffered many things of many physicians, had spent all that she had, and was nothing bettered, but rather grew worse."**

Imagine twelve years of being impoverished by spending all her savings and earnings on medical bills and sanitary pads until she heard of Jesus. The Bible did not tell us if she was a married woman or a spinster. Whatever her marital status, the condition must have affected the bliss in her marriage or the prospect of a happy wedlock.

Jesus knows those who are reaching out to him in faith.

Her Healing

The Bible says that faith comes by hearing. This woman heard of Jesus. She heard of the miracles of healing and deliverance He had performed. *"If this man could heal a mad man, the deaf and dumb, the blind and crippled people, He should be able to heal my haemorrhage,"* she must have said to herself, *"but how do I reach Him*

The Woman with the Issue of Blood

amidst this crowd? Will He know how desperately I need his prayers for my healing?"

As a ritually unclean person, she should be avoided to prevent contamination (Leviticus 15: 19 – 23). Hence, she did not expect Jesus to touch her. Where there is a will, there is always a way. This woman was determined to get her miracle and she devised a means – she would do the touching, touching at least the hem of his garment. Perhaps she heard the miracles of Jesus among the people of Gennesaret who begged to touch the hem of his garment as recorded in Mathew 14: 34- 36. "And as many as touched were made perfectly whole" This woman had faith and was desperate for her healing. She took the initiative on how to get to Jesus and as soon as she got close enough to him through the crowd, she reached out in faith. The healing was instantaneous. The flow stopped and she knew it. Jesus also knew it. He knew that healing virtue had been transmitted from his body in response to faith.

Reactions

> "And Jesus, immediately knowing in himself that virtue had gone out of him, turned him about in the press, and said, Who touched my clothes?
> And his disciples said unto him, Thou seest the multitude thronging thee, and sayest thou, Who touched me? And he looked round about to see her that had done this thing (Mark 5: 30 -32).

There is a difference between thronging and touching. The disciples were surprised that the Master could be asking for who touched him amidst the crowd who were pressing on Him from all directions. Many crowds attend miracle services today but only few go with a heart full of faith to receive their desired miracles. Jesus knows those who are reaching out to him in faith. Jesus knew that power, healing virtue flowed out of him to accomplish a healing in response to a touch of faith. He also knew who touched him and for what purpose. He just wanted the woman to acknowledge the receipt of her healing and testify so that it may be confirmed. There is power in declaring the testimony of what God has done, it is one of the weapons to overcome the enemy.

The Woman with the Issue of Blood

"And they overcame him by the blood of the Lamb, and by the word of their testimony…" (Revelation 12: 11a)

"But the woman fearing and trembling, knowing what was done in her, came and fell down before him, and told him all the truth. And he said unto her, Daughter, thy faith hath made thee whole; go in peace, and be whole of thy plague" (Mark 5: 33 -34).

This woman was overwhelmed by the instant solution to a problem of twelve years that had defied different medications. She trembled by the contact with the awesome power of the astonishing Christ. She was afraid of the publicity but she could not be hid. She had to open up and confess or testify of all that happened. Jesus confirmed her healing and declared peace and wholeness to her life. It is good to exercise faith in Jesus. Jesus called this woman "Daughter" because of her faith. Anyone who wants to be a daughter or son of Jesus must demonstrate faith in Him. It is through our faith that we become children of God (Gal.3:26). Without faith, it is impossible to please God (Hebrews 11: 6).

Beneficiaries of Grace

There is healing power in Jesus and it can be contacted by faith. Whatever the length or the depth of your problem, the duration or the magnitude of your medical condition, by putting your faith in Jesus, this Jesus Christ who is the same yesterday, today and forever, you will surely be overwhelmed by how easily his healing power will put a permanent stop to the unpalatable condition. May you experience His healing as you reach out to touch Him by faith (Amen).

Anyone who wants to be a daughter or son of Jesus must demonstrate faith in Him. It is through our faith that we become children of God.

Personal Application

Faith in Jesus still works wonders today and does not **necessarily** have to be transmitted through any medium like cloths, handkerchiefs, water, oil or any object. His power can still be contacted to work miracles of healing today through faith in His Name. Until you get desperate to get a solution out of a problem, the idea that will birth a miracle may not be conceived and the needed steps will not be taken. *"Take heed what you hear"* (Mark 4:24a). This woman heard of Jesus and took steps that led to the transformation of her life. What are you hearing when in one problem or the other? You have heard of Jesus but what step of faith have you taken to become a beneficiary of His grace? Are you among the multitudes thronging to church without a definite encounter with Jesus to transform your life from all uncleanness? I dare you to reach out in faith and touch Him today.

Faith in Jesus still works wonders today and does not necessarily have to be transmitted through any medium like cloths, handkerchiefs, water, oil or any object.

CHAPTER THREE

THE DAUGHTER OF JAIRUS

Enjoying the Faith of a Father

The healing of the woman with the issue of blood was sandwiched between the account of the healing of Jairus' daughter as recorded in Mark 5: 21- 24 and 35- 43. It could also be found in the other synoptic gospels, Matthew and Luke.

> *"And when Jesus was passed over by ship unto the other side, much people gathered unto him: and he was nigh unto the sea. And, behold, there cometh one of the rulers of the synagogue, Jairus by name; and when he saw him, he fell at his feet. And besought him greatly, saying, My little daughter lieth at the point of death: I pray thee, come and lay thy hands on her, that she may be healed; and she shall live. And Jesus went with him; and much people followed him, and thronged him.*

While he yet spake, there came from the ruler of the synagogue's house certain which said, Thy daughter is dead: why troublest thou the Master any further? As soon as Jesus heard the word that was spoken, he saith unto the ruler of the synagogue, Be not afraid, only believe. And he suffered no man to follow him save Peter, James, and John brother of James. And he cometh to the house of the ruler of the synagogue, and seeth the tumult, and them that wept and wailed greatly. And when he was come in, he saith unto them, Why make ye this ado, and weep? The damsel is not dead, but sleepeth.

And they laughed him to scorn. But when he had put them all out, he taketh the father and the mother of the damsel, and them that were with him, and entered in where the damsel was lying. And he took the damsel by the hand, and said unto her, Talitha cumi; which is, being interpreted, Damsel, I say unto thee, arise.

And straightway the damsel arose, and walked; for she was of the age of twelve years. And they were astonished with great astonishment. And he charged them straitly that no man should know it; and commanded that something should be given her to eat."

The Daughter of Jairus

The Faith of a Father

The name of the recipient or beneficiary of this healing was not recorded, but that of her father was. She got her healing through the faith of her father, Jarius, a ruler of the local synagogue in the town where the miracle took place. Jairus could be likened to an elder or pastor in today's church settings. He might be one of the Pharisees. He displayed great humility by falling at Jesus' feet begging Him to heal his daughter despite his position as the ruler of the synagogue. He was unlike the other ruler of the synagogue who got angry at Jesus for healing on a Sabbath.

Jairus demonstrated faith in Jesus' power to heal and spoke in faith concerning the condition of his daughter. He believed that the touch of Jesus' hands was what was needed to keep her from dying. When faced with critical health challenges, it is important to confess positively about the situation. There is power in words, as the scripture says:

> *"Death and life are in the power of the tongue...."* (Proverbs 18:21a)

> *"And when he saw him, he fell at his feet and besought him greatly, saying, My little daughter*

lieth at the point of death: I pray thee, come and lay thy hands on her, that she may be healed; ***and she shall live***". (Mark 5: 23)

Jesus honoured the faith of Jairus by going with Him to his house. Remember Jesus just crossed over from the other side of the sea; he just came back from a journey. Yet, he agreed to follow Jairus, trekking the distance. This was a gracious act and revealed the kind-heartedness of Jesus. He was and is always available to everyone who call on him in faith. Even if he delayed like in the case of Lazarus in John 11, he would always show up at just the right time.

The Messenger and the Mourners

Before Jesus got to the house, a messenger brought news of the death of the child to Jairus while he was still talking with Jesus. The messenger was of the opinion that Jairus should not bother bringing Jesus since the child had died. **Why trouble the Master?** Death is the end of all and it has come to Jairus' daughter. Jesus did not allow the news to register in the conscious mind of Jairus long enough to weaken his faith but quickly countered it with positive words of assurance **"Be not afraid, only believe"**. Faith is like a plant, it can wither if exposed to adverse conditions. We all need to keep our faith in Jesus alive for him to be able to demonstrate his power in our lives and situations. There is no situation that is beyond the power of Jesus. Perhaps Jesus had not raised any dead as at this point in time and that may have been the reason why the messenger saw no need to trouble the Master. Jesus encouraged Jairus' faith by telling him not to be afraid.

Fear is the opposite of faith. Once you are with Jesus, the Alpha and Omega, the one whom the grave cannot hold captive, there is no cause for fear. Bible scholars said that there are 366 "fear not" in the Bible which means everyday of the year we are to exercise faith not fear, whatever the circumstance. May we not receive evil tidings or message in Jesus' name. Even in the face of evil tidings (such as news of the death of a loved one, negative medical report, loss of a contract or job opportunity, denial of promotion, visa or admission etc.) Psalms 112:7 says: ***"He shall not be afraid of evil tidings: his heart is fixed, trusting in the Lord."*** Faith in God will counter the side effects any evil tidings may have on one and when God sees the faith in one's heart, He will turn the sorrow into joy in

His own way and time. So, Jesus is still saying *"Fear not, only believe."*

Meanwhile, a crowd of mourners had gathered in Jairus' house on the passing away of the twelve year old daughter. Mourners have no faith in Jesus, instead they laughed him to scorn when he said that the child was only sleeping.

> *And he cometh to the house of the ruler of the synagogue, and seeth the tumult, and them that wept and wailed greatly. And when he was come in, he saith unto them, Why make ye this ado, and weep? The damsel is not dead, but sleepeth.* (Mark 5: 38 - 39)

Mourners have a way of making a mountain out of a mole hill. They help to exaggerate the problem beyond hope of solution. They help one to focus on the problem and doubt the possibility of any solution even by Jesus intervention. They cannot see through the eyes of faith to believe that with God, nothing shall be impossible. Mourners are specialists in sympathizing with one's tragedy; they don't know how to rejoice when good things happen. That is why Jesus had to put them all out before the healing and strictly charged

The Daughter of Jairus

Jairus not to tell them after the miracle has been performed. They make much ado about nothing.

Some people are like that today even in the church, they always feel sorry for your calamity and help you feel like bemoaning your woes. They don't inspire faith in you through positive words of encouragement but only make you feel miserable with their greetings of condolences. Don't be surprised that when your miracle finally comes, you may not see them coming around to rejoice with you the way they have always been around to mourn your situation. Mourners don't celebrate; remove them from your circle of friends because voice of joy and thanksgiving is what will be resounding in your house in Jesus' name. Wallowing in self-pity or calling a pity party to bemoan your calamity will definitely not proffer a solution to the problem. Instead, get people of faith to go in with you to challenge the problem as Jesus did. Jesus removed the mourners so as not to dampen the faith of Mr and Mrs Jairus. The insincerity of the mourners could be seen through their laughing at Jesus. How could one wail and weep and also laugh at the same time? Mourners always make a mockery of Jesus and his power to heal or deliver from any unpleasant situation.

And they laughed him to scorn. But when he had put them all out, he taketh the father and the mother of the damsel, and them that were with him, and entered in where the damsel was lying.
(Mark 5: 40)

Faith is like a plant, it can wither if exposed to adverse conditions.

The Healing and Reaction

The healing of Jairus daughter was performed through the gracious touch of Jesus' hands and his voice declaring "Arise". Jesus delivered this girl from the cold hands of death by touching her with his hands that is full of life and power. He touched and spoke with authority at the same time. Note the **"I say unto thee"**. The author of life was the one speaking here. And what did he say? "**Arise**." Yes, arise from deathbed and walk. Arise and live; grow to

The Daughter of Jairus

womanhood and fulfil God's purpose in life. Arise and Shine. The death of a child does not help to fulfil God's purpose for the child, so she must arise. And she arose and walked and ate.

> *And he took the damsel by the hand, and said unto her, Talitha cumi; which is, being interpreted, Damsel, I say unto thee, arise. And straightway the damsel arose, and walked; for she was of the age of twelve years. And they were astonished with great astonishment. And he charged them straitly that no man should know it; and commanded that something should be given her to eat.* (Mark 5: 41 - 43)

The healing or the raising was instantaneous like most of Jesus' miracles. There was great astonishment; everybody present in the room was shocked; that is, the parents and the three disciples. This could have been the first miracle of raising the dead performed by Jesus known to them. This young lady became one of the beneficiaries of the abundant grace of God in that though the world had given up on her; Jesus did not give up on her. He has come to give life and that abundantly (John 10:10). She received life back to fulfil divine purpose and became a spectacle of

God's grace. Thank God she had a Dad who dared to seek, beg and believe in Jesus. Glory!

Personal Application

How far can you go to get Jesus' attention for a family member in one problem or the other? Are you afraid of evil tidings? Let not your heart be troubled, only believe in God. Are you surrounded by pity party and mourners? Put them out and turn your eyes of faith on Jesus. Whatever is dead in your life, health, finance, marriage, career, business, spiritual life, name it, can arise and walk again. All you need is a touch or voice of Jesus, the Lord of Life. Dry bones shall live again for all things are possible with God. Only believe.

How far can you go to get Jesus' attention for a family member in one problem or the other?

CHAPTER FOUR

THE DAUGHTER OF THE SYROPHENICIAN WOMAN

Blessed With a Persistent Mum

The biblical record of this healing or deliverance from demons according to Matthew 15: 21- 28 reads:

"Then Jesus went thence, and departed into the coasts of Tyre and Sidon. And, behold, a woman of Canaan came out of the same coasts, and cried unto him, saying, Have mercy on me, O Lord, thou son of David; my daughter is grievously vexed with a devil.

But he answered her not a word. And his disciples came and besought him, saying, Send her away; for she crieth after us. But he answered and said, I am not sent but unto the lost sheep of the house of Israel.

Then came she and worshipped him, saying, Lord, help me. But he answered and said, It is not meet to take the children's bread, and to cast it to dogs. And she said, Truth, Lord: yet the dogs eat of the crumbs which fall from their masters' table. Then Jesus answered and said unto her, O woman, great is thy faith: be it unto thee even as thou wilt. And her daughter was made whole from that very hour."

The Request

This is a unique case of grace that flowed across racial and social boundaries and barriers and made the unqualified to be qualified. By her status, right from birth, the Syrophenician woman was disqualified from being a beneficiary of grace, an alien from the commonwealth of Israel (Eph.2:12). She however looked beyond the ancient barriers and standing order of cultural and spiritual limitations. She dared to ask to be a beneficiary of the inexhaustible grace that does not discriminate. Grace flowed down and took her up from the status of a dog to enjoy out of the benefits of a son.

The work of deliverance performed by Jesus in this account was a generous show of the grace of Jesus. The request for help came from a Canaanite woman who knew who Jesus was. Canaanites were enemies of

The Daughter of the Syrophenician Woman

the Israelites; the Israelites warned by God not to have any dealings, either business, marriage or any social interaction with them. In fact, the Israelites waged wars to eradicate them from the promise land (Judges 1: 1- 4). This woman was an enemy of the Jews and yet she came to Jesus for help. She called him the son of David. She knew the lineage of Jesus and the history of the Jews. She knew they were merciful people and had heard of the power of Jesus to perform miracles. She did not allow racial and social barriers to hinder her from coming to Jesus.

This woman had but one request – **mercy**. She cried for mercy and help because her daughter was under demonic oppression. Mercy makes you get what you do not deserve. She knew she had no right to talk to Jesus, much less even asking him for a favour. She needed mercy and was desperate to be helped by Jesus. No other cure existed for demonic oppression but the power of Jesus. She was determined to get an answer to her cry for mercy and so kept following and crying after Jesus and the disciples even when Jesus did not answer a word. Note that this woman did not ask Jesus to have mercy on her daughter. She knew that her child's woe is equal to her own woe. This shows the heart of a true mother. Her daughter's healing is her healing, so she is the one in need of mercy. The lyrics of a song say:

> *It's me, it's me, it's me o Lord,*
> *standing in the need of prayer*
> *It's me, it's me, it's me o Lord,*
> *standing in the need of prayer*
> *Not my father, not my mother,*
> *but it's me o Lord, standing in the need of prayer.*
>
> *It's me, it's me, it's me o Lord,*
> *standing in the need of prayer.*
> *Not my brother, not my sister*
> *but it's me o Lord, standing in the need of prayer*
>
> *It's me, it's me, it's me o Lord,*
> *standing in the need of prayer.*

Contrary to the idea behind this song which sounds self-centred, this woman took her daughter's need as her own personal problem.

The Golden Silence

There are times when God is silent. To a child of God, his silence can be frustrating and confusing. Does he not care that we perish? Is his love for us gone forever? No wonder David wrote:

> *"Unto thee will I cry, O Lord my rock; be not silent to me: lest, if thou be silent to me, I become like them that go down into the pit".* (Psalm 28:1)

Asaph also revealed how desperately we all need to hear God speak when we are in unpalatable situations:

> *"Keep not thou silence, O God: hold not thy peace, and be not still, O God".* (Psalm 83:1)

God can decide to keep silent or speak in whatever situation we are passing through. When He speaks, we are assured that he has not forgotten us. Even when he chooses to keep silent too, his love for us is unchanging. A child of God should not doubt the Father's love when he chooses to remain silent over a troubling circumstance. We should not begin to ask questions like the disciples on the stormy sea, ***"Careth thou not that we perish?"***

Jesus did not answer this woman because she was not a child of the kingdom. He had no obligation to respond to her plea. He knew his purpose and audience. He was sent to the house of Israel, not Canaanites. Contrast this cry for mercy with that of Bartimaeus, the blind man on the road to Jericho in Mark 10: 46 - 52 who said the same thing: *"Jesus, thou son of David, have mercy on me"*. Verse 49 says Jesus stood still and commanded him to be called. A cry for mercy from a child of the kingdom cannot go unanswered. Jesus **must** do something about your situation if you are his child. We were all like this woman at a time in our lives. We were not a people worthy to receive the least of his grace, but He found us out and lifted us up. Ephesians 2: 12 makes it clear:

> *"That at that time ye were without Christ, being aliens from the commonwealth of Israel and strangers from the covenants of promise, having no hope, and without God in the world."*

The Power of Worship, Humility and Persistence

What you cannot get through supplications, prayers and intercessions can be got through thanksgiving and worship (1Tim. 2:1). This woman

The Daughter of the Syrophenician Woman

was making supplication, prayer and intercession for her daughter but to no avail. Then she switched over to worship before making her request for help again and the answer began to come. She came near to Jesus and bowed down or knelt down in worship. She did not mind the dust or the onlookers. These are factors some of us consider that prevent us from giving quality worship and praises in church today: *"My fine cloth will be dirty or what will people think of me?"* This woman did not mind these factors, she knelt down and worshipped Jesus and then asked for help the second time. It was after this that Jesus answered her and in words which could be counted as demeaning. Yet her humility and persistence saw her through. She didn't mind being referred to as a dog, she was content to get just a crumb of the children's food.

Namaan in his encounter with Prophet Elisha almost lost his opportunity to be healed of leprosy through pride. He was not humble enough to follow the divine prescription by the prophet to dip himself in the Jordan River seven times (2Kings 5: 9-14). He too was an alien to the commonwealth of Israel yet he claimed supremacy of the rivers in his own country over River Jordan. Thank God that he did not come alone. If not for his servants, he would have returned angrily to Syria and perhaps died a leper. Many people miss their miracles of healing and breakthrough today because of pride. Beneficiaries of grace must be humble. God resists the proud but he gives grace to the humble (1Pet.5:5b, James 4:6).

Children versus Dog

A child is a potential heir of the parents' property. He or she has access to all that belongs to the parents even in their lifetime. A child as an offspring is an extension of the parents and takes after them in look, behaviour, physique, attitude, voice, gesture to mention a few. A dog on the other hand is not a human part of the family however long it has stayed or whatever fondness it has enjoyed. Usually dogs are meant to stay outside the house (especially in our continent) while children have a room in the house (Rev. 22:15). Calling someone a dog is derogatory. Nobody likes to be treated as a dog. Goliath the giant Philistine hated to see David come to him with a stick and exclaimed "Am I a dog that thou comest to me with staves?"(1Sam.17: 43). Actually he was a "dog" because he was an alien to the commonwealth of Israel. Anyone who has no portion in the covenant blessing of God through faith in Christ today is also a stranger and a "dog" (Eph. 2:12; Phil. 3:2). The question is "Are you a child or a dog?" Now there are some children who don't know their rights as children of God, hence they are still feeding on crumbs when they should be enjoying the riches of the glory of the inheritance (Gal.4: 1-7 and Eph. 1: 17 – 18).

Faith and Healing

Most if not all of the healings and deliverances performed by Jesus were in response to the faith of the recipients or that of an intermediary who sought Jesus on behalf of the beneficiary. Faith is the current through which the power of God flows to people to transform their unpleasant situations. Without faith, it is impossible to please God (Heb.11:6).

> *"Then Jesus answered and said unto her, O woman, great is thy faith: be it unto thee even as thou wilt. And her daughter was made whole from that very hour".*

Jesus always commented on people's level of faith. To the disciples on the stormy sea he said *"Why are ye fearful, O ye of little faith"* (Matthew 8: 26) but to this woman and some others whose level of faith impressed him, he said *"Great is thy faith"* (Matthew 15: 28). People of great faith always receive their hearts' desires. The daughter of this woman was delivered immediately. As soon as Jesus spoke, the demons disappeared out of her and she was made whole. Even demons tremble at the sound of his voice because the voice of the Lord is powerful. May His voice come into every situation of your life and grant your heart's desires as you exercise great faith in the mighty name of Jesus.

Faith is the current through which the power of God flows to people to transform their unpleasant situations.

The Daughter of the Syrophenician Woman

Personal Application

Are you sure you are not an alien to the commonwealth of Israel? You are not entitled to enjoy the privileges of the kingdom yet if you are an alien. Healing is one of the rights of the kingdom people. First things must come first. Receive Jesus into your life and be saved from your sins. Then your cry for mercy will definitely receive a reply. As a child of the kingdom, are you enjoying to the maximum all the entitlements of the kingdom? As a mother, how far can you go for the lives of your children? Are you desperate enough to attract heaven's attention over the life of that child the devil is trying to possess? Jesus will always respond to the cry of a persistent mother.

CHAPTER FIVE

THE MOTHER-IN-LAW OF SIMON PETER
Laid Down but Raised To Serve

The account of this healing is taken from Matthew 8: 14 and 15. It is a very short account yet reveals a lot about the gracious personality of Jesus.

> *"And when Jesus was come into Peter's house, he saw his wife's mother laid, and sick of a fever. And he touched her hand, and the fever left her: and she arose, and ministered unto them."*

This account can also be found in the other synoptic gospels. Luke 4: 38 and 39 reads:

> *"And he arose out of the synagogue, and entered into Simon's house. And Simon's wife's mother was taken with a great fever; and they besought him for her. And he stood over her, and rebuked*

the fever; and it left her; and immediately she arose and ministered unto them."

Jesus will not think it a waste of his power if you go ahead to ask him to heal you so you can perform your duties at home, workplace and in the church better.

The Itinerant Teacher

Before considering the work of grace done in the life of Peter's mother-in-law, there is something important to note about this Jesus of Nazareth. Mathew 4: 23 -25 records how he went all about the province of Galilee, teaching in their synagogues as well as preaching and healing all manners of sickness and diseases among the people. His fame spread to many regions beyond Galilee, to Syria, Decapolis,

Jerusalem in Judea and beyond the Jordan River and multitudes of people followed him. There was no radio or television at this time, no channels such as CNN (Cable News Network) or BBC (British Broadcasting Corporation) to showcase the healing crusades, yet his fame spread to other countries.

When Jesus saw this multitude, he went up into a mountain and sat down. He did not mean to escape from the multitude but to get a better platform to teach. When he was set, his disciples came to him and he taught them the longest teaching recorded in the Bible which has been tagged the Sermon on the Mountain. The mountain was his pulpit and only God knows how his voice could reach the audience without a public address system. He did not teach only his disciples who came up to the mountain with him. Chapter eight verses twenty eight and twenty nine read: *"And it came to pass, when Jesus had ended these sayings, the people were astonished at his doctrine; for he taught them as one having authority and not as the scribes"*.

The people also listened and were surprised about his teachings. The first part of the teaching was tagged the Beatitudes and entails the required attitudes or dispositions of anyone who wants to enter into the kingdom of heaven. It includes poverty of spirit, mourning, meekness, hunger and thirst for righteousness, mercy, purity of heart, peace-making and enduring persecution for righteousness sake (Mat. 5:3-12). Other topics of his teaching centred on:

- being a light and salt (13-16),
- his fulfilment of the law and prophets (17-19)
- the need to be more righteous than the scribes and Pharisees in order to enter the Kingdom of heaven (20). Pharisees and scribes were the keepers of religious instructions. They helped the people to understand the Law as delivered through Moses. However their lifestyles were full of hypocrisy, double standard and covetousness. Jesus therefore went on to explain:
- the sixth commandment- thou shall not kill (21-26),
- the seventh commandment- thou shall not commit adultery (27-32)
- and other details of the old testament doctrine on swearing (33-37),
- taking revenge (38-42),
- loving others (43-48).

He went on in chapter 6 to teach them:
- acceptable standards of giving to the poor (Mat 6: 1- 4),
- the model of acceptable prayer (5-13),
- the need for forgiveness (14- 15)
- the right disposition to fasting (16 -18),
- money matters and proper investment medium (19-20),
- the correlation between treasure and heart (21)
- the danger of covetousness or evil eye (22-23),
- the impossibility of serving God and money (24),
- how to avoid anxiety about insufficient finances to feed and clothe (25- 34).

The last chapter of the sermon or teaching in chapter 7 of Matthew
- warns against fault-finding and being judgmental (1-5),
- the need to keep your precious things or treasures from those who don't value them (6),
- the assurance of a loving heavenly Father answering our prayer requests (7-11) and
- a summary of the law and prophets - ***do to others as you want them to do to you*** (12).

As an expert teacher, Jesus concluded his teaching by using sets of words and opposites to drive home his teaching –
- the narrow and wide gates,
- the sheep and the wolves,
- the good and evil trees and their fruits,
- the wise and foolish builders (13-27).

It was a long but soul-lifting teaching and the people saw the difference in Jesus teaching and that of the scribes. He is the Word personified (John 1:1). On coming down from the mountain, Jesus continued healing the people. He healed a leper and a servant of an army officer that was sick of palsy. His coming to Peter's house was probably to rest and have some food after the long teaching and healing sessions. On getting there, there was another healing to perform, Grandma had a fever.

Just a Fever

Peter, unlike the centurion, had not invited Jesus to his house (8:5-7) to come and heal his mother-in-law. It was on getting there that he saw her sick and lying down with a fever. Perhaps, having a fever was not a big issue like palsy or leprosy, to have warranted

The Mother-In-Law of Simon Peter

inviting Jesus to handle. It could be just a malaria fever that will go after taking some herbs and having enough rest. This means it was a minor case - just a fever. Jesus dealt with both minor and major cases of illness. Jesus healed her through the touch of his hands according to Matthew's account. Luke says he rebuked the fever and it left her. Immediately the hands of Jesus touched hers, the fever disappeared. She **arose** and **ministered** unto them by perhaps cooking a delicious meal.

Every sickness has a name and can flee at the sound of Jesus' voice or the mention of his name today by believers. Any sickness that will not make one to arise but lie down is not in God's plan for His children. Many people in church today who are familiar with Jesus like Peter see their *fever* as not big enough to demand divine intervention. Yet that condition is limiting their usefulness or productivity in God's vineyard. It could be a malaria fever, cough and catarrh, sprain, menstrual pain, head ache, tooth ache, back ache, eye disease and so on. Jesus will not think it a waste of his power if you go ahead to ask him to heal you so you can perform your duties at home, workplace and in the church better. Recipients or beneficiaries of Jesus grace should serve him by using their new life and energy to minister unto Him.

Recipients or beneficiaries of Jesus grace should serve him by using their new life and energy to minister unto Him.

Personal Application

Don't let that "fever" hold you down from serving the Master. Rise up and minister to the Lord with the abilities He has given you. *No situation is too small to invite Jesus to handle. Let Him help you take charge of those little things that throw you off balance* and minimize your usefulness in your home, workplace or church.

CHAPTER SIX

MARY MAGDALENE

Transformed and Ever Loving

The first mention of Mary Magdalene was in respect of her support of Jesus ministry. The details of her deliverance from demon possession was not recorded anywhere in the Bible. Luke 8: 1 – 3 revealed the supporters or sponsors of Jesus' ministry which interestingly were mainly women.

> *"And it came to pass afterward, that he went throughout every city and village, preaching and shewing the glad tidings of the kingdom of God: and the twelve were with him, And certain women, which had been healed of evil spirits and infirmities, Mary called Magdalene, out of whom went seven devils; And Joanna, the wife of Chuza, Herod's steward, and Susanna, and many others, which ministered unto him of their substance."*

Beneficiaries of Grace

Beneficiaries Are Supporters

The supporters or sponsors of Jesus' ministry were many and could not all be mentioned. No ministry succeeds without supporters either with human or material resources. Jesus chose the twelve to be with him (human resources) but he also needed financiers though he could bring money out of the mouth of a fish. Top among the supporters of Jesus were Mary Magdalene, Joanna and Susanna. Apart from the fact that they supported him with their resources, they followed him on his ministerial tours into towns and villages. Jesus was not a city preacher; neither was he a rural pastor. He "**went *throughout every city and village, preaching and shewing the glad tidings of the kingdom of God***" (Luke 8:1).

These women had been healed or delivered by him at one point or the other and so were showering Jesus with support and affection which women are usually good at expressing. Mary Magdalene (that is from Magdala) showed greatest expression of gratitude to Jesus because she had experienced the greatest deliverance. She was possessed with seven demons and Jesus had cast them all out of her. She was changed, transformed, free and totally liberated. Although the episode of her deliverance was not narrated by any of the gospels, her experience of an encounter with Jesus was no doubt validated by the quantum of love she displayed for her Lord. Being demon possessed by seven evil spirits would have been a horrible experience. Her case may be similar to that of the mad man of Gadara who was possessed by a legion of demons. With such an experience, it was doubtful if she was married or had children. She was miserable and tormented by the devil, a social outcast, yet, she became one of the beneficiaries of grace. There is no one so deep in sin or so possessed with demons that the grace of Jesus cannot reach. Jesus is still transforming prostitutes, adulterers, fornicators, armed-robbers, assassins, witches, demonic herbalists, occults, drug addicts and everyone under the shackle of sin today.

After her deliverance, Mary loved the Lord with passion. She could give anything to him to express her gratitude. She loved much because she was forgiven much. No wonder she could spend of her resources to support the ministry of Jesus. Many so-called Christians today find it hard to support the work of God. The reason perhaps may be that they have not really experienced in-depth the love and grace of Jesus. Anyone who has had an encounter with this man of

Galilee will surely find a way of expressing love for him in appreciation. This will take us to consider the event that happened in Luke 7: 36 - 50 when Jesus was guest at a dinner in the house of Simon, a Pharisee. While he was at table, a woman came in and began to wash his feet with her tears and dried them with her long hair. Different thoughts sprang up within the host, the Pharisee as to the authenticity of Jesus' holiness and power. The Lord knowing his thoughts rebuked him for his lack of display of love by not even giving Jesus water to wash his dusty feet when he entered. The crux of the story is that beneficiaries of grace are people of love. They love the Lord and people too. Not only that, they also display their love no matter the reactions of the watching world. They can sing:

> *We will worship the Lamb of glory,*
> *We will worship the King of kings,*
> *We will worship the Lamb of glory,*
> *We will worship the King,*
>
> *And with our hands lifted up,*
> *we will worship and sing,*
> *And with our hands lifted up,*
> *we come before him rejoicing,*

With our hands lifted up to the sky
while the world wonders why,
We just tell them we are loving our King,
oh, oh, oh,
We just tell them we are loving our King.

So, as a beneficiary of grace, what have you done in the recent time to display your love for the Lord Jesus? True beneficiaries of grace don't care what the world will think or say about their devotion to the Lord. Go ahead and love him if you have truly experienced his saving grace.

What we do for the Lord will surely be long remembered after we have even died and gone to glory.

The Outcome: Always with Jesus

Mary was there at the trial and crucifixion of Jesus. When the twelve deserted him for fear of being arrested along with Jesus, Mary and the other women who loved the Lord were at every scene (Matthew 27:55 – 56). They watched him as he was beaten by the Roman soldiers with such brutality that made them shiver with horror. They watched as they nailed his hands and feet to the old rugged cross. They watched him bleed to death and give up the ghost. When his ribs were pierced with a spear and blood mixed with water gushed out, they kept watching and wailing. What a miserable way to die! "This man was too good to die like this", they must have thought. Little did they know that He was being wounded for our transgression, bruised for our iniquity, that the chastisement of our peace was upon him and that by his stripes, we were healed! (Isaiah 53: 5).

Mary Magdalene with the other women watched as the soldiers brought him down from the cross and Joseph of Arimathea and Nicodemus, silent disciples of Jesus carried him to be buried in the tomb of the rich. It was a tomb carved out in a rock which Joseph had prepared for himself. This was another beneficiary of grace who did not mind giving up his richly prepared burial place for the Lord. Little did he know that the body of Jesus will only lie there for two nights and that on the third day the tomb will be empty. Empty and yet it became a centre of attraction for tourists and pilgrims every year for over two thousand years later. What we do for the Lord will surely be long remembered after we have even died and gone to glory. The women wanted to embalm the body of Jesus so it would last long before decay. Early on Sunday morning, they were at the grave with spices and ointments which they had bought on the evening of the Sabbath. They just want to be with Jesus, both in life and in death.

It was with grieving hearts that they went to the grave. They were almost there before they remembered the big stone rolled over the entrance of the cave. "Who shall help us roll away the stone?" They went on anyway and got to the tomb to meet the greatest surprise of their lives (and of history). The stone was already rolled away but the body of Jesus was also taken away.

That is one of the attributes of beneficiaries of grace - they are "possibilitarians." All things are possible to those who believe. When they remembered the obstacle of the stone, they had the option of going back on the way, but they did not. That is faith. Most of the things we fear or worry about are actually not real or have been handled by God even before we get to the junction. The stone is gone and the Lord is risen.

Commissioned To Share the Good News

John's account of the resurrection story revealed much to us about the love of Mary for Jesus. Read John 20: 1 – 18. When Mary discovered the empty tomb, she ran to Peter's house to inform him. Both Peter and John ran to the tomb to verify her claim. The body is gone of a truth. Who could have taken it? They went back home to reason that out, being men (rational beings). What is the use of staying with an empty grave when the Lord's body is not there? After Peter and John had gone back home in confusion over what could have happened, and perhaps to hide from being seen by the soldiers who crucified Jesus, Mary remained at the tomb. She stood outside the tomb weeping. Women of a truth are emotional beings. She wept and wept not even afraid of the scary environment of a tomb.

Now, we all know a burial place has some awe and bloodcurdling feelings, yet she waited there alone weeping. Mary's love for Jesus had removed every iota of fear from her even at the sight of the angels. No wonder the Bible says that perfect love casts out fear. When she bent to see again where the body laid, she saw two angels.

> *"And they say unto her, Woman, why weepest thou? She saith unto them, Because they have taken away my Lord, and I know not where they have laid him"* (John 20:13).

Was she really expecting to see Jesus alive again? Not too likely. Was she just too grief-stricken at the death and disappearance of her Lord's body? Probably yes. The spices were still in her hands but of no use anymore. Then she saw the risen Lord and would have hugged him. When Jesus appeared to her, she was commissioned to carry the good news to others:

> *"Jesus saith unto her, Touch me not; for I am not yet ascended to my Father: but go to my brethren, and say unto them, I ascend unto my Father, and your Father; and to my God, and your God"* (John 20:17).

Mary enjoyed the special grace of seeing the Master even before He appeared before the Father. Not even Peter or John could enjoy this benefit. Mary who was once possessed with seven horrible demons and lived a miserable life, far from the kingdom life; now brought by grace right into the kingdom to be the first person to see the risen Lord, the embodiment of grace. Your past life should not be an obstacle to enjoying the benefit of seeing the Lord at his return. His grace can count anyone with a miserable past worthy of a glorious tomorrow. That is what grace does.

What a privilege for Mary to see the Lord again, not his corpse to anoint or embalm but his glorious resurrected body. Halleluyah he is alive and forevermore. Death could not hold him captive; even in the grave, Jesus is Lord. Note that Jesus referred to the disciples as brethren, not disciples. This is one of the benefits of the resurrection: we are made joint-heirs with Christ. We have access to the Father as much as Jesus, and He is our God. All beneficiaries of grace have equally been commissioned to share the good news of what Jesus has accomplished for humanity. It is good news and must be shared. We are in an era of grace, a season of God's goodwill to mankind and so cannot afford to keep quiet if truly we have benefited from his grace.

Personal Application

If you have been delivered by the Lord Jesus from the hold of the devil, you should express your love for Him like Mary Magdalene did. How much of your resources, time, energy, influence are you willing to spend for the Master's course? Support the gospel so that others may hear and be delivered from the hold of the devil. Do you really love Jesus? Can your priorities in life show that you love Him most affectionately?

Beneficiaries of Grace

All beneficiaries of grace have equally been commissioned to share the good news of what Jesus has accomplished for humanity.

CHAPTER SEVEN

THE SAMARITAN WOMAN
Thirsty for Satisfaction

This is an account of another beneficiary of grace who was transformed from being a social outcast to an evangelist. The story of this woman of Samaria can be found only in the Gospel of John chapter four, verse one to forty two. Jesus must go through Samaria on his way to Galilee and had a stop-over at Sychar.

> *"Then cometh he to a city of Samaria, which is called Sychar, near to the parcel of ground that Jacob gave to his son Joseph.*
>
> *Now Jacob's well was there. Jesus therefore, being wearied with his journey, sat thus on the well: and it was about the sixth hour.*

Beneficiaries of Grace

There cometh a woman of Samaria to draw water: Jesus saith unto her, Give me to drink. (For his disciples were gone away unto the city to buy meat.)

Then saith the woman of Samaria unto him, How is it that thou, being a Jew, askest drink of me, which I am a woman of Samaria? For the Jews have no dealings with the Samaritans. Jesus answered and said unto her, if thou knewest the gift of God, and who it is that saith to thee, Give me to drink; thou wouldest have asked of him, and he would have given thee living water.

The woman saith unto him, Sir, thou hast nothing to draw with, and the well is deep: from whence then hast thou that living water? Art thou greater than our father Jacob, which gave us the well, and drank thereof himself, and his children, and his cattle?

Jesus answered and said unto her, Whosoever drinketh of this water shall thirst again: But whosoever drinketh of the water that I shall give him shall never thirst; but the water that I shall give him shall be in him a well of water springing up into everlasting life. The woman saith unto him, Sir, give me this water, that I thirst not, neither come hither to draw.

Jesus saith unto her, Go, call thy husband, and come hither. The woman answered and said, I have no husband. Jesus said unto her, Thou hast well said, I have no husband: For thou hast had five husbands; and he whom thou now hast is not thy husband: in that saidst thou truly" (John 4:5-18).

Her Social Status

The woman in consideration was a Samaritan. Samaritans were regarded by the Jews as second-class citizens because of their mixed religious worship (See 2Kings 17: 24-41). This Samaritan woman was not happily married as she had had five husbands and living with the sixth man. This condition would have made her women folks to despise her because of her unstable marriage. Any woman who leaves her husband and marries another is adulterous according to biblical standard. So, she was a Grade A adulteress and also a Samaritan - double social outcast. No wonder she came to the well alone and at such an odd hour of the day. Women and girls usually go in groups to the stream or well in the evenings or early mornings. She might have decided to come alone at an odd hour to avoid the gossips and slanderous looks from other women in the village. She might not have had a friend because every man would have warned his wife not to befriend such a woman.

Why would a woman jump from one man to another up to six men? Different plausible answers could include childlessness, sexual promiscuity, maltreatment from husband, bad or hot temper and lack of submission which is vital for a woman to display in her matrimony. Whatever was the cause of her predicament, this woman agreed that she had no husband. She was a freelance wife, ready to jump out of matrimony for the slightest reason. And that was the point of her life at which Jesus caught her attention. Jesus had asked her for a drink and she was yet to give him. Instead, she had engaged him in series of interrogation to know why a Jew would want Samaritan water. Jesus was not a racist and would have drunk the water if she had offered it. This woman must have been so used to being a social outcast that she was surprised that a Jewish man would ask her for a drink. Or perhaps she thought that Jesus was like one of those men from which she had jumped from one to another.

Although she did not give Jesus water to drink, she was ready to collect his water which she thought would quench her physical thirst so she would not need to come to fetch water again. How selfish and gullible! Won't she still need water for cooking, washing, bathing and other domestic uses of water? Jesus however did not rebuke her selfishness or laugh at her stupid reason for wanting the living water. His giving is not give-and-take kind of giving and he understands our very need even if we don't know the right words to use to describe them.

The Gracious Gift of God

God is a giver. He gives and gives again and again. No man can out give God. He gives even when we don't deserve it. His giving is gracious, not dependent upon our righteousness.

> *"….for He maketh his sun to rise on the evil and on the good, and sendeth rain on the just and on the unjust"* (Matthew 5:45b).

He gives us even when we are stingy and won't give to him in return or to our fellow men. His greatest gift was given when we were most unworthy.

"But God commendeth his love toward us, in that, while we were yet sinners, Christ died for us." (Romans 5:8).

"For God so loved the world that He gave his only begotten Son, that whosoever believe in him should not perish but have everlasting life" (John 3:16).

"Jesus answered and said unto her, if thou knewest the gift of God, and who it is that saith to thee, Give me to drink; thou wouldest have asked of him, and he would have given thee living water" (John 4:10).

Jesus is God's greatest gift to humanity. The only one qualified to take away our sins (Math 1:21). Unfortunately most people do not know this gift of God. They try different religions to gain access to and get approval of God. Yet the one and only way to God is Jesus. He says of himself in John 14: 6:

"I am the way, the truth and the life; no man cometh unto the Father, but by me".

Jesus is the way and is available for as many as are wandering hopelessly in the wilderness of life. His grace is available to as many as would tap into it and ask him. This Samaritan woman did not know the grace of Jesus. She had no idea who was asking her for water, yet she made her request - *"Sir, give me this water."* That is the requirement to become a beneficiary of grace. It's yours for the asking.

> *"For there is no difference between the Jew and the Greek: for the same Lord over all is rich unto all that call upon him. For whosoever shall call upon the name of the Lord shall be saved"* (Romans 10:12-13).

Just ask him to save and deliver you from your sins and you are in for a glorious experience of transformation as this woman. The salvation that Jesus brings is like a well of water that never dries. He invites all who are thirsty to come and drink of the well of salvation. See John 7: 37 – 39, Isaiah 12:3, Revelation 22:17. Bring your cup and ask Jesus, the gracious gift of God to fill it up for you. He says **"*thou wouldest have asked of him, and he would have given thee living water*"** (John 4:10).

Ask and you shall receive till your cup is full and you want no more as in the song:
Fill my cup, Lord; I lift it up Lord,
Come and quench the thirsting of my soul,
Bread of heaven, fill me till I want no more,
Fill my cup, fill it up and make me whole.

The Transformation

The living water quenches spiritual thirst, not physical one. The longing for sin, the desire to commit adultery and other sins would be gone once this woman drank of the living water of salvation. The living water washes sinners clean and quenches the thirst for sin. It breaks the power of sinful addiction whatever the length or depth of its hold on the sinner. Halleluyah! But Jesus put a condition for the woman to enjoy the living water. Why did she need to call her husband? The first husband was the real husband, she had to retrace her steps. This signifies the need for repentance and restitution in order to enjoy the living water. Every sinner must acknowledge his or her sinful state and be ready to repent and make necessary restitutions.

The woman admitted that she had no husband which was the truth. She acknowledged her sinful state by saying the number six man is not her husband. Divorce is not in God's original plan for marriage. When Jesus through word of knowledge told her the number of men she had had, her spiritual consciousness was awakened and she commented:

> "……Sir, I perceive that thou art a prophet. Our fathers worshipped in this mountain; and ye say, that in Jerusalem is the place where men ought to worship." (John 4:19-20).

To this, Jesus explained that true worship has nothing to do with location but should be in spirit and in truth. He made it known that God is seeking for true worshippers. Her response and his declaration were in verses 25 – 26.

> "The woman saith unto him, I know that Messias cometh, which is called Christ: when he is come, he will tell us all things. Jesus saith unto her, I that speak unto thee am he.

Jesus helped her faith by declaring his identity as the Messaiah which he never did to the Pharisees even when they asked him to tell them plainly if he was the Christ. The disciples were surprised but asked no questions when they came back and saw him discussing with a woman, a Samaritan for that matter.

> *"The woman then left her water pot, and went her way into the city, and saith unto the men, Come, see a man, which told me all things that ever I did: is not this the Christ? Then they went out of the city, and came unto him* (verse 28-30)
>
> *And many of the Samaritans of that city believed on him for the saying of the woman, which testified, He told me all that ever I did.*
>
> *So when the Samaritans were come unto him, they besought him that he would tarry with them: and he abode there two days. And many more believed because of his own word; And said unto the woman, Now we believe, not because of thy saying: for we have heard him ourselves, and know that this is indeed the Christ, the Saviour of the world."* (John 4:39-42)

It was a great transformation for this woman. Her spiritual perception and head knowledge that a Messiah was coming combined to arouse her interest in knowing the personality of the man speaking to her. She forsook all by leaving her water pot to become a mouthpiece for Jesus. She testified of Jesus' power to know all her past and invited the men to come and see. Note that she invited the men, not the women. She knew her audience, the people she could easily capture their attention and the result was tremendous. Many believed on Jesus because of her and also much more when they heard Jesus for themselves.

That is what every beneficiary of grace is expected to do. Tell others what Jesus has done for you, invite them to Jesus and let them have a personal conviction of Jesus as the Saviour of the world. The Samaritan woman was an instrument in the hands of God to reach her people with the gospel. No matter the past life of a sinner, there is no limit to what God can do through one who accepts Jesus Christ and forsakes all to follow him. Although there was no mention of the life of this woman after the incidence, she would no doubt stop her adulterous lifestyle and perhaps be reunited to her first husband and lived together happily ever after.

Personal Application

Many people troop to the church today because of physical water instead of the spiritual or living water. Are you asking Jesus for physical needs only without the quenching of your soul's thirst by the living water? An encounter with Jesus will transform you and make you abandon your water pot of worldly pursuits for satisfaction, for a higher calling. Redirect the ability you had used in the past to capture souls for the devil to now capture souls for Jesus henceforth. Identify your right audience for ministry and the result will be tremendous. Do you have only a report about Jesus as the Messiah and are yet to experience His transforming power in your life? The time is now, why delay any further? Let God find you as one of the true worshippers.

Tell others what Jesus has done for you, invite them to Jesus and let them have a personal conviction of Jesus as the Saviour of the world.

CHAPTER EIGHT

THE WOMAN CAUGHT IN ADULTERY
Saved To Sin No More

This story displays one of the most important works of grace in the Bible. The woman in question enjoyed salvation from physical death as well as eternal condemnation. Her story could be found in John 8: 1-11.

> *"Jesus went unto the Mount of Olives. And early in the morning he came again into the temple, and he sat down, and taught them. And the Scribes and Pharisees brought unto him a woman taken in adultery, and when they had set her in the midst, They saith unto him, Master, this woman was taken in adultery, in the very act. Now Moses in the Law commanded us, that such should be stoned: but what sayest thou?*

This they said, tempting him, that they might have to accuse him. But Jesus stooped down, and with his finger wrote on the ground, as though he heard them not. So when they continue asking him, he lifted up himself, and said unto them, He that is without sin among you, let him first cast a stone at her. And again he stooped down and wrote on the ground.

And they which heard it, being convicted by their own conscience went out one by one, beginning at the eldest even unto the last: and Jesus was left alone and the woman standing in the midst.

When Jesus had lifted up himself, and saw none but the woman, he said unto her, Woman, where are those thine accusers? Hath no man condemned thee?

She said, No man, Lord. And Jesus said unto her, Neither do I condemn thee: go, and sin no more."

Adultery Then and Now

The seventh commandment is a warning against adultery. Adultery is a sexual sin and can be committed by both married men and women. It is an act of unfaithfulness to the marriage vows. It is a sin against one's partner and also against God. It is worthy of death among the people of Israel in the Old Testament era and up to the time of Jesus' earthly ministry as found in this account. Leviticus 20: 10 - 21 is a list of the various sexual sins that can be committed which includes adultery with a neighbour's wife, stepmother, daughter-in-law, aunty, sister-in-law, homosexuality, bestiality and incest. There are different punishments attached to these sins.

    Both married men and women are expected to remain faithful to each other until death parts them. However, this issue of adultery has been an age-long problem plaguing the society and perpetrated by both the rich and the poor, educated and illiterates, kings and servants, employers and employees. King David despite being the man after God's heart was dented by this sin of adultery. In this age, adultery has become like a fashionable or normal thing among unbelievers. It is branded as having extramarital affairs as if it is an extracurricular activity. Sad to say, even some Christians are falling into the snare of this deadly sin through carelessness and overindulgence with the opposite sex. May God have mercy.

> *"Nevertheless, the foundation of God stands sure having this seal, the Lord knoweth those that are his and let everyone that nameth the name of Christ depart from iniquity"* (1Timothy 2:20).

The Gender Bias

This woman (which some Bible commentaries say may be Susanna) was caught in the very act of committing adultery. In the very act means right in the middle of the action with both the man and the woman caught together, perhaps on the bed or mat, naked. The accusers brought only the woman and not the two of them. Leviticus 20:10 says both of them must be killed, but the interpreters of the law were partial and brought only the woman. Why? Could the man have bribed his way out? Could he be a highly placed person or even a fellow Pharisee? Whatever the reason, they were ready to stone the woman. They came stone in hand to Jesus and brought the woman too for him to see and condemn before they stone her to death. They wanted to see if his own teaching will contradict the Law of Moses (which they have not fully obeyed) so they can have an accusation against him. **Women have often been subjugated and at the receiving end of many** *societal ills.* This woman was worthy of death indeed but what of her partner in sin?

Compare this episode with that of Zimri, an Israelite from the tribe of Simeon and Cozbi, a Midianite woman who went in to a tent to commit immorality right in the presence of the people of God. Phinehas, the grandson of Aaron the High Priest went to them in the tent and killed both of them in the very act by thrusting a javelin through their bodies. He did not spare the man, he was just and fair in executing his judgment. God blessed him for this holy zeal to end iniquity in the camp by establishing a covenant of peace with him (Numbers 25:1 – 15). He was not gender-biased, to kill only the foreign woman. That was a holy and impartial zeal.

The Law and Grace

The Teachers of the Law wanted to trap Jesus with their question – "The Law says this, what do you say? The Law and Grace do not speak the same thing. John 1:17 says *"The law was given by Moses but grace and truth came by Jesus Christ"*. The law criticises and condemns while grace commends, the law kills while grace saves. The law says *"You have sinned and should die"*, but grace says *"You have sinned but your sins are forgiven, go and sin no more."* The work of grace is to deliver us from the power of sin, not give us a license to commit sin. That is why one should beware of preachers today who preach that one can commit sin and still be holy. Apostle Paul wrote extensively to the Roman church on this matter of grace and sin. See Romans 6: 1- 23 especially verse 15:

> *"What then? Shall we sin, because we are not under the law, but under grace? God forbid".*

We should not receive the grace of God in vain but grow in it (Heb 6:1-8, 2 Pet 3:18).

The work of grace is to deliver us from the power of sin, not give us a license to commit sin.

"Go and Sin No More"

The accusers of this woman wanted her to die. They pestered Jesus with their question on his view of the sinfulness of this woman. Then the Master said, "let him who has not committed any sin throw the first stone." Any sin, not only adultery because all sins are equal before God. Many of us even Christians usually attach greater gravity to immoral sins and excuse lying and pride. However the Bible says **"All unrighteousness is sin"** (1John 5:17a) A lie is equal to murder or adultery and disobedience is like witchcraft in God's eyes. So, let us stop justifying some sins while condemning others. It is not the nature of Christ.

When none of the accusers could claim righteousness and left one by one beginning from the oldest, the woman was left alone. Jesus lifted up himself and asked if no one had been able to condemn her. Then he said, **"Neither do I condemn you, go and sin no more"**. Jesus was righteous because he had no sin and was qualified to pass the judgment. Instead he chose to pardon, justify, discharge and acquit her. She was saved from the penalty. The Son of Man has come to save the world and not to condemn it. This woman received the power to go and sin no more. Surely, she won't go back to that sin partner who abandoned her to death nor to any other man apart from her husband. What a grace! It is a second chance to live again because she would have been killed that day. So, this woman lived supporting Jesus' ministry with her new life and resources (Luke 8:3).

Personal Application

Are you misusing the grace of Jesus by indulging in sin? Are you a partial judge condemning one sin while excusing another? Are you condemned by the society, family or the church because of your wayward life? Hear Jesus: **"Neither do I condemn you, go and sin no more."** No matter how bad you are, Jesus loves you but hates the sin in you. Let Him give you the power to go and sin no more. He is a Saviour now but will soon be a Judge.

> *"He that believeth on him is not condemned: but he that believeth not is condemned already, because he hath not believed in the name of the only begotten Son of God"* (John 3:18).

CHAPTER NINE

MY PERSONAL TESTIMONY

"And of His fullness have all we received, and grace for grace" - John 1: 16

This book will be incomplete without putting my personal testimony of how I have benefited from the grace of Jesus. His grace has lifted me from death to life, from sickness to health, from sorrow to joy, from sin to righteousness and from darkness into His marvellous light. I have enjoyed the grace of Jesus in every aspect of my life: physical (academics, career, finance, health, marriage and family life) and above all spiritual.

I invited Jesus into my life to be my Lord and Saviour on the 31st of December 1988. It was a decision that transformed my life. Knowing Him has brought many blessings upon blessings and grace for grace into my life. I could see His guiding hands in both major and minor details of my life. For the purpose of this book, I will be concentrating on the grace of healing I enjoyed from Him.

Like the lyrics of that song "It is truly wonderful what the Lord has done":

> *There is not a single blessing,*
> *which we receive on earth,*
> *That does not come from heaven,*
> *the source of our new birth.*
>
> *It is truly wonderful what the Lord has done*
> *It is truly wonderful, it is truly wonderful,*
> *It is truly wonderful what the Lord has done*
> *Glory to His name.*

Psalm 126: 3 says *"The Lord hath done great things for us; whereof we are glad."*

> *The Lord hath done great things for us and*
> *we are filled with joy!*
>
> *The Lord hath done great things for us and*
> *we are filled with joy!*

*The Lord hath done great things for us and
we are filled with joy!*

The Health Challenge

It all started on a beautiful Saturday morning in August 2015. I woke up to find a lump in my left breast. It was small, painless and fixed, that is, not a mobile type of lump. I was breastfeeding my last baby who was seventeen months old then. I kept feeling it with my hands and hoping it would go away just as it had gone away some five years earlier when I was breastfeeding my second baby. It refused to go and I told my husband about it. We prayed as we always do and he advised me to see a doctor in the University Health Centre. I weaned my baby the following month and went to the Health Centre in October from where I was referred to the then State Specialists' Hospital in Akure. The doctor asked me to do a test called "fine needle aspiration" which involved insertion of a needle to take a sample of the lump. The result came out "inconclusive" as no tangible evidence of cancer was seen. I was asked to go for lumpectomy, which is the removal of the lump from the breast. This was done in November and the whole lump (about 4cm) taken to the histology laboratory for further test. I was told to come back in two weeks. I didn't want to go but my husband encouraged me. I went after three weeks, which was already mid-December. I didn't want to go for the result because I thought that was the end since the lump has been removed. I had no iota of doubt in my heart that the result would be negative. But alas, I was unprepared for the result which revealed that the lump was an invasive carcinoma.

My husband and I were both shaken by the news. My mind was racing! I was so overconfident before but the news shattering. *How come? Why me? What next? Would I have to be taken to India for treatment? How much would it cost?* These were some of the questions racing through my troubled mind. It was two weeks to Christmas. When everyone was going for shopping and planning special cooking for the end of year, I was going to the hospital to see an oncologist for a solution to my predicament.

Thank God for doctors, they always have medical routes to almost every health challenge. So it was that I took my first dose of chemotherapy on the 23rd of December, 2015. The nausea and loss of appetite that followed did not let me enjoy that Christmas dish which I had to cook for my family. The second dose followed after three weeks. This time, the nausea and loss of appetite was accompanied with vomiting and my hairs started falling off. Even though I had cut the last hairstyle I did to low cut after Christmas and bought a new wig, the remaining were falling like snowflakes from my head.

By the time I took the third dose on the first of February, 2016, the chemicals had weakened me so much that for three days I couldn't eat any solid thing. I vomited even ordinary watermelon and fruits that I managed to eat. I would just lie on the bed weak and unable to go beyond the house for a whole week. Then I started having red and itchy eyes like "Apollo" [conjunctivitis]. My fingers nails and toe nails all turned black, as if black ink was injected into them. It wasn't a pleasant experience. Meanwhile, the oncologist said I would have to take six courses. I wondered – if I had taken three and I had turned out like this, what would happen by the sixth dose?

Thank God for Pastors. My Daddy in the Lord, Pastor (Prof.) S.O. Ewuola visited me the week of the third dose. We didn't tell him earlier until when he noticed my absence in the church during the January monthly prayers and enquired. He prayed with us and told us that as he entered our sitting room, the Lord told him that this sickness was not unto death. Halleluyah! I have come to know him as a mouthpiece of God for my life from past experiences. (Previously, he told me to start buying baby things in December 2006 after waiting for two years and three months for another conception after we lost our first baby who was almost clocking two years when he died then. Approximately nine months later I had my Promised baby). Based on this premise, when God told us through him that this sickness was not unto death, I believed it wholeheartedly. So if this breast cancer was not unto death, and this chemotherapy was almost killing me, I had better stopped it. I had little or no information then about alternative medicine, but I just reasoned that I wouldn't let this chemo kill me. *"God said it, I believe it and that settles it."*

I said "bye" to chemo and to my dear oncologist. She advised me to take just one more dose and that she would write in my case note that my inability to tolerate the drugs was the reason I quitted. I begged her to understand with me and since a doctor can't force a patient, she wished me well (not without giving me cases of people who would abscond and later come back when it was beyond repairs). I didn't like the awful effects of chemotherapy and therefore chose to believe the word of God and live. Now, I love celebrating birthdays and my 40th birthday (which I had been eagerly looking forward to) was just three months away. I detested the idea of still taking chemo few weeks to my birthday. I would rather hold on to God.

I later got to know of and purchased some health products from various companies. These were used between February and December 2016. I accidentally met an acquaintance who told me of a supplement called *Cellgevity* produced by Max company. We met briefly in passing somewhere on the FUTA campus on the first Saturday of December and she told me that she had something to tell me about a seminar. I promised to see her in her shop where I normally buy storybooks for my children. I didn't really put it on my priority list the following week until I had a dream one afternoon that I needed to go and find out what she had to tell me. (I have learnt from past experiences to take my dreams seriously, especially dreams in the afternoon). So I went and she said she wanted to invite me for a seminar. I thought she wanted to invite me for a Christian youth or teenagers' seminar. When she said it was a health seminar of one product, I didn't really like the idea but then I remembered the dream. So I agreed to just go and hear about the product. The testimonies from the product seminar were fantastic, so I decided to key in to the Max benefits of health and wealth. I used it for about three months and stopped because the price was a bit on the high side and I felt I was okay.

The Second Phase

I continued normal life and took the supplement once in a while. As the year 2017 was going to an end, I was in for another surprise. The lump came back in multiples, about three or four in the same left breast. I notified my husband and he was of the opinion that we just go and remove the whole breast. That didn't go well with me. I told him to let me try using the supplement again and see if the lumps would go. I started using it massively in January 2018. Meanwhile, I noticed I usually had an ache on the right side of my head every month since November 2017. It would last for about five days and go, only to return the following month. By February, my husband encouraged me to ask questions from one of our daddies in the church who is a medical doctor. At that time, the ache was getting to my eyes and right ear. He advised me to see another doctor in the church who is an eye specialist which I did. In short, I started using glasses and the eye ache reduced. When he asked of my medical history and I told him of the previous experience, he made me realize that the breast should have been removed initially and that the head ache could be linked to breast cancer spreading to them.

I later observed about a month later that anytime I did normal chores, all my bones would begin to ache as if I had been using an axe on wood. By April 2018, the bone ache was gaining momentum in frequency and intensity. I started using pain relievers prescribed by a doctor in the University Health Centre. Also, as I was driving on the 5th of April, taking my children for a camp meeting, I just noticed that I was seeing doubly. I had to close one eye so that I could focus with the other eye. If I watched TV, all the images on the screen doubled. In no time, my left eye was like squinting. The iris with the pupil (the black centre of the eye) would not move to the side if I rolled the eyeballs. It was just stationary in the middle. I asked the eye doctor to examine the eyes and the result showed that the nerves in the eyes as well as the face

Beneficiaries of Grace

were weak. He asked me to do my mouth as if I wanted to blow a balloon, but alas, I couldn't do it.

By May, the bone aches had become a constant - k, so much that I was always taking pain relievers in either tablet or injection form. We were connected to a surgeon and booked the surgery for the end of May, 2018. Meanwhile, I let the doctor do a tissue biopsy just to confirm if the lump was still cancerous as I was in no hurry to lose my breast. The result came out to be a Stage Two Invasive Carcinoma. By the 29th May, which was a public holiday, I woke up with pains all over, found it difficult to bend and walking was slow and painful. I had to be rushed very early before dawn to the hospital to first relieve the pains and later to the other clinic around 7am for the surgery which took place the next day. My husband was not even around that day, but I thank God the brethren took up the responsibility. They arranged for prayer networks, donation of blood and initial cash deposit for the surgery. The support was massive in all dimensions- spiritual, financial, material and human. When my husband came later that day, he prayed with me and encouraged me not to fear because *"this sickness is not unto death."* We kept holding on to the word from the Lord of over two years before. It became our slogan.

My Personal Testimony

And so it was that I went in for the mastectomy on 30th May, 2018. In all, I took six pints of blood during and after the operation. The doctor expressed his pleasant surprise after the operation. With the facial distortion due to failure of facial nerves, he was expecting to see a very advanced level of decay and spread of the cancerous cells to the chest but thank God it was not to be. I was in the hospital for two weeks.

I appreciate the leader and members of the Women's Fellowship of the Chapel of Faith, Federal University of Technology, Akure (FUTA) for sleeping on chairs in the hospital with me, bringing various types of dishes, fruits and water. I salute the Daddies and the Chapel Youth Fellowship Executives for their support. I am grateful to the Chairman and members of the Chapel Council and all the medical doctors and nurses in the Chapel who rendered their professional services free of charge at different stages. How can I thank my fathers and mothers, brothers and sisters from the Gospel Faith Mission International enough, my nuclear and extended family members and all friends and acquaintances who came visiting for the support? My noble colleagues including my Head of Department and my Dean, all rose up to support me. How can I forget the immense contribution of the Vice

Chancellor and his wife, or the support received from the Academic Staff Union of University (ASUU) FUTA Branch during this time? I am so blessed to have such massive support. God bless everyone.

After being discharged from the hospital, I was lodged in the University Scholars' Lodge for another two weeks to recuperate. I discovered I was unable to toilet for about ten days. Also, my right leg was bending at the knees like that of an old woman with osteoporosis. My right ear was also buzzing or making noise endlessly. It was at this point I experienced the supernatural dimension of healing. I experienced divine healing of my leg that was bending through a simple prayer by a man of God. It was on Sunday, 17th June, 2018 and it was Fathers' Day celebration at the Chapel. The guest minister, Pastor Joshua Odeyemi came to visit me at the lodge when he asked of me from my husband. He encouraged us and prayed a very simple prayer. I called it simple because he was not rebuking and casting out the "spirit of cancer". I was not really expecting any specific or dramatic touch but I just believed this prayer will add to the contents of the prayer bowl that people had been praying for me and I trusted God to see me through the experience.

My Personal Testimony

One of the mothers in the church, a nurse at the University Health Centre was also present to dress the wound. After the pastor left with my husband and she finished the dressing, I told her about the bending of the knee. I got up to walk around the room to let her see what I meant. To my amazement, the leg was no more bending at the knee. I walked faster round the room, it has gone. I screamed as I was over-joyous!

    I left her in the room walking as fast as never before. She locked the door after me and followed me out of the lodge, I walked up and down in front of the lodge, full of joy and exercising my faith in the healing before the devil would come with his lies that it was not real. She told me to take it easy and not stress myself. So, I asked her to bring a chair out so I could sit and enjoy the sunlight and still walk as much as I wanted after resting. I had never experienced such joy, such gratitude, singing with tears flowing from eyes as I sat there after she had gone, basking in not only the warm sunshine of the morning but also in the love of the One who loved me so much that by His stripes I was healed. I am a living witness and beneficiary of His grace.

This miracle gave me so much confidence that God who healed this leg would also heal other parts. He would not waste his healing virtue on me, but perfect all my health. Why God chose to heal the leg I could not explain, but I thought it was because I needed the leg to go places in the course of other treatments. Remember, my left eye was still squinting, my right ear buzzing, the bone pain had not gone and the wound from the surgery had not healed up. At this time my husband got me a music box and downloaded some healing messages and plenty songs on my phone to keep my company and strengthen my spirit. I so much cherished how the songs of Tope Alabi (*Halleluyah, Ta Lo Dabi Re, You are Worthy* etc) and those of Sola Allyson (*Mo Juba, Iba, Iyin, Adun* etc) blessed my spirit. It was a time of retreat for me even though I couldn't pray much.

Various suggestions of herbal treatments came in at this time. I appreciate the suggestions of the University Registrar, Mr. R. A. Arifalo, who is well-experienced in that regard. The Vice Chancellor also got me a supply of herbal capsules and ointment that had proved useful in treating breast cancer and boosting immunity. Through a sister, I got to know her friend, who was a breast cancer survivor. She came visiting at the lodge with another member of the Team Survivors Nigeria and the Breast Cancer Association of Nigeria (BRECAN). They encouraged me and also suggested other medicinal plants. They helped me blend elephant grass and one other bitter plants to help with the bowel movement. I also ordered for green tea and after ten days of no bowel movement, I was able to toilet again. This is a blessing we normally take for granted. My distorted face started going back to normal with the herbal treatments and supplements. I also started eating a lot of fruits and vegetables which I still keep up till date.

After leaving the lodge, my husband decided we needed to go for CT scan of the head to know what was making noise in the ear. We were linked through one of our doctors in the Chapel to Ondo where I did the scan on the 3rd July, 2018. The x-ray and written report were scary. At this time, a team of doctors plus the Chairman of Chapel Council set up to make contact with my former oncologist to know the next line of action. She graciously advised them that I go for radiation at the University College Hospital (UCH) Ibadan and wrote a referral note to a colleague there.

The experience at UCH was another eye-opener to the suffering of humanity in the hands of sickness and to the failure of our government in the health sector.

My husband got his annual leave for August to stay with me and we spent three weeks in Ibadan. On the first day at the hospital, we were able to see a doctor around 3pm and went to do various blood tests to ensure I could undergo the radiation. I brought the results of the blood test and the CT scan the next clinic day. The medical students from the University of Ibadan were to have a class with the consultant in his office that day. So he displayed the x-ray film of the scan on a screen with white light to illuminate the film and asked one of them, a lady to explain it. It was scarier as the light illuminated it to show how the cancerous cells had spread to my skull and especially at the right side. For the first time I was scared as the magnitude of the situation dawned on me. But immediately I remembered the words of David that ***"what time I am afraid, I will trust in thee."*** (Psalm 56:3). The students were looking pitifully at me. I fought back the tears and then the doctor gave a reassuring smile that calmed me and made me force a smile. He said the case was an emergency and quickly took me to the radiation room to book an appointment.

My Personal Testimony

Now, a lot of patients were already booked and it would have been around December before I could get a space. One woman came from Auchi and was asked to come back in September before she could get a space. But with God's favour and the emergency case, I was asked to start the next Thursday, which was 9th August. I would be having three courses of the radiation on the back and he marked where to focus the rays on my lower spine. The waiting room for the radiation was like the pool of Bethesda, in Bible days, filled with impotent folks of men and women, young and old, citizens and foreigners. One woman came from Cameroon and said the radiation machine in Nigeria was better. Can you imagine one machine serving the whole southern Nigeria and beyond!

I was just praying (selfishly) that it won't breakdown before I completed my treatment. I am most grateful to God for seeing me through that phase. I cannot forget to appreciate the family of Pastor Ologbonyo Richard with whom we stayed for the three weeks in Ibadan. He accommodated us, drove us on each appointment day at the hospital and stayed throughout. There was a day we didn't leave the hospital until almost 8 p. m., and had been there since around 10 a. m. I am also grateful to everyone God raised up to take care of my children at home, and all colleagues who took up my official work while on sick leave.

The radiation was done to the back and not the head and so the doctor said I would need a "little" chemotherapy. Come and see people sitting for hours on chairs in doctor's office taking chemotherapy (maybe there was no enough provision for bed spaces). I told him I would prefer to go and have it in Akure so he gave me another note referring me back to my oncologist in Akure. She gave me two weeks break to recover from the effect of the radiation before starting chemotherapy. The bone pains reduced drastically after the radiation remaining the buzzing ear and the squinting eye which was gradually getting normal. There were fears on every side about the chemotherapy that it destroys both good and cancerous cells and that the success rate is low. With prayers and generous use of supplements to boost my immunity, I scaled through the six doses with minimal discomfort. Let me say here that the reason for high mortality rate from chemotherapy is that the immune system gets compromised by the chemicals. Hence, it will be safe to take immune boosting supplements

My Personal Testimony

before, during and after chemotherapy. Also, so many people spiritualise cancer and take to casting out the "spirit of cancer" without taking other treatments. God heals cancers just like any other diseases but the prerogative for the healing method to use lies with Him. Doctors care but God cures, Pastors pray but God heals. I use this opportunity to thank all men and women of God who prayed for me.

Throughout the period of taking the chemo, there was no vomiting, nausea and general weakness. There was only a little loss of appetite and running stomach for a day or two after taking it and of course loss of hair. The blackness of nails was very minimal too compared to the previous one. The oncologist recommended a higher brand of chemotherapy drug produced in America which was costly but had little side effect. Each course was over a hundred thousand naira but I thank God for supplying all my needs according to his riches in Christ Jesus. I completed the courses and also took some bone injections monthly to strengthen the bones. I bless God for seeing me through it all. His grace carried me through. He supplied every need for my healing through supernatural, medical and herbal methods. I am not better than those who died from cancer; it was just His grace I benefited from. I am bold to say that I am one of the Beneficiaries of Grace.

Let me say here that the reason for high mortality rate from chemotherapy is that the immune system gets compromised by the chemicals. Hence, it will be safe to take immune boosting supplements before, during and after chemotherapy.

Three Healing Dimensions
> "Is there no balm in Gilead; is there no physician there? Why then is not the health of the daughter of my people recovered? (Jeremiah 8: 22)

My Personal Testimony

Doctors have a slogan that says "We care, God cures". When God wants to cure someone, he can do it through supernatural means by prayer. He can use natural means or medical means. He can also combine any of the two or even the three methods. God reserves the prerogative as to which method to employ in healing someone. God is not against the work of physicians or doctors. He gave them the wisdom to treat various ailments. Neither is He against the use of drugs as He is the creator of whatever is used to prepare the drugs. He owns both the balm and the physician.

When King Hezekiah was sick unto death, God showed him through Prophet Isaiah the herbs (figs) to pluck that healed the sickness that was almost killing him (Isaiah 38:21). The prophet did not pray for Hezekiah, neither did Elisha pray for Naaman before his leprosy disappeared. He was told to just dip himself seven times in River Jordan and his skin was healed and fresh as that of a baby (2 Kings 5:14). On the other hand, the woman with the issue of blood had spent all her savings on physicians and was getting worse until she encountered Jesus. Jesus healed several blind men using different styles. He healed some instantly and another he healed progressively. He mixed clay with saliva and rubbed on one and told him to go and wash and he came back seeing while he spit on the eyes of another and he saw men walking like trees and he had to repeat it till he saw clearly. Yet others he simply healed according to their faith without spitting, rubbing clay or washing (John 9:6-7, Mark 8:23-24, Matt. 9: 27- 30).

Jesus is still a healer today, no matter the advance level of breakthrough in science and medicine. He heals not only the body but also the soul and spirit. Only Doctor Jesus can heal and deliver from demonic oppression. Only he can cure the soul from sin. What a wonderful Saviour is Jesus my Lord.

God is not against the work of physicians or doctors. He gave them the wisdom to treat various ailments.

CHAPTER TEN

FINAL WORDS

Reading through the stories of women who lived in the time of Jesus and benefited from his abundant grace, would have given more insight into the personality of Jesus. He has a big heart so full of love that he went to the cross to die for the sins that were not committed by him but by you and me. He chose to die for us not because we deserved it but because of his grace. Have you received of his grace? Are you one of the beneficiaries of His grace? His grace brings healing, deliverance from demonic oppression, transformation from social and psychological inferiority complexes, salvation from the power of sin and of course prosperity. 1 Corinthians 8:9 says

Beneficiaries of Grace

"For ye know the grace of our Lord Jesus Christ, that, though he was rich, yet for your sakes he became poor, that ye through his poverty might be rich".

The GRACE of Jesus is abundant and non-discriminatory (John 1:16, 10:10). It is all-sufficient for every situation (2 Cor.12:9). Here are some of the things the Grace of our Lord Jesus can do in a life. It can lift someone
- from sinfulness to holiness (Rom. 5:17),
- from sickness to health (1Pet. 2:24),
- from bondage to freedom (John 8:32, 36),
- from poverty to wealth (2Cor. 8:9) and
- from death to life (Eph.2: 4, 5).

The grace of Jesus Christ is all encompassing. He can **make** you to become what you ought to be.

Are you a daughter or son of the kingdom and still bowed down by powers and circumstances beyond your control thus making you live as a shadow of your real self? Arise and be loosed by the voice of Jesus proclaiming liberty to you: "Woman, thou art loosed".

Final Words

Are you a child and yet feeding on crumbs like the dogs? Begin to possess your possession of healing and good health as from today.

Are you haunted by your past life and think your case is a write off? You are just the right candidate to experience grace.

Are you blocked by barriers of religion or social class and think you dare not cross the boundaries? Reach out to him in faith and he will receive you no matter who you are.

Are you still struggling with sin even though you are professing to be a Christian? Then receive the power to go and sin no more through the grace and truth that came by Jesus.

If you are yet to experience the work of grace in your life and a stranger to the commonwealth of Israel, then you need to invite him into your life to become a beneficiary of his grace. Like the Samaritan woman, ask him to give you the living water and he will do. He will quench every thirst and give you full satisfaction in life.

According to Blaise Pascal, *"There is a vacuum in the heart of every man which only God can fill with his Son Jesus Christ"*. Become totally liberated and free indeed.

"If the son shall make you free, you shall be free indeed" John 8: 32.

Have you received his grace for salvation? Then tap into other graces too - good health, wealth, peace and dominion. Remain in Him and continue to enjoy the benefits of His grace.

> *May the grace of the Lord Jesus Christ, the love of God and the communion of the Holy Spirit be with us all. Amen* (2 Corinthians 13: 14).

www.ingramcontent.com/pod-product-compliance
Lightning Source LLC
Chambersburg PA
CBHW031448040426
42444CB00007B/1022